Collaborative Business Design:
The Fundamentals

Improving and innovating the design
of IT-driven business services

Collaborative Business Design:
The Fundamentals

Improving and innovating the design of IT-driven business services

Brian Johnson

Léon-Paul de Rouw

IT Governance Publishing

Every possible effort has been made to ensure that the information contained in this book is accurate at the time of going to press, and the publisher and the author cannot accept responsibility for any errors or omissions, however caused. Any opinions expressed in this book are those of the author, not the publisher. Websites identified are for reference only, not endorsement, and any website visits are at the reader's own risk. No responsibility for loss or damage occasioned to any person acting, or refraining from action, as a result of the material in this publication can be accepted by the publisher or the author.

IT Governance Publishing Limited
Unit 3, Clive Court
Bartholomew's Walk
Cambridgeshire Business Park
Ely
Cambridgeshire
CB7 4EA
United Kingdom
www.itgovernancepublishing.co.uk

First published in the United Kingdom in 2018
by IT Governance Publishing:

ISBN 978-1-84928-976-4

FOREWORD

In this guide, we have set out the fundamentals of an approach to collaborative business service design. The approach will assist both the demand and supply sides (and the SRO) to address the principal needs and drivers that set the requirements, conditions, outputs and outcomes for robust IT-driven services that properly support the business. This approach is rooted in the dynamics of the business stakeholders and focuses on IT-driven services that are fit for purpose.

Who made us the experts? No one. We have not reinvented any best practice wheels or thinking, nor have we altered existing best practices. The approach is based on well-established service design thinking and an extension of that thinking to embrace existing best practices such as PRINCE2®, Gateway®, P30® and many others. Joining up these practices led to a simple and pragmatic approach that becomes a tool to focus on the alliance between the business and IT. This is extensively discussed and presented in our book published by ITGP, *Collaborative Business Design; Improving and innovating the design of IT-driven business services[1]*.

But sometimes you just need a handbook and a few instructions that focus on the essentials. And this is presented in the book you have here: Collaborative Business Design: The fundamentals. This guide illustrates

---

[1] *www.itgovernance.co.uk/shop/product/collaborative-business-design*

to you how to use the approach and come up with a service design brief. This 'Service Design Statement' as we call it, will guide and help you to navigate the IT-driven business service lifecycle.

You can find more instructions and insights in our blog at ITWNET, and of course the website of ITGP[2]. More information about training opportunities and discussions is available on the ITWNET website[3].

We hope CBSD supports you in improving the development, building and servicing of IT-driven business services in your organisations.

Brian Johnson

Léon-Paul de Rouw

---

[2] *www.itgovernancepublishing.co.uk*

[3] *www.itwnet.com/groups*

CONTENTS

Contents

Contents

x

1. IT-DRIVEN BUSINESS SERVICES

Outside of a dog, a book is man's best friend. Inside of a dog, it's too dark to read.

Groucho Marx

1.1 Business need and value

The primary focus of this guide (with respect to the fundamentals of collaborative business service design) is the needs of the business; what information must be collected, how IT is processed, what is automated, can be automated, can never be automated, what is the result we want, how will this new service be paid for and what (if any) income is required from it.

As such, it is imperative to understand the characteristics of IT-driven services and service offerings. We need to understand the service requirements and to describe a structured approach to gather the right requirements for effective service solutions.

Rarely, however, do business managers pay the same attention to making sure the service they need is designed according to all their requirements and constraints (such as regulatory constraints, for example). This lack of attention leads to a poor customer experience. However, such an omission is often unintentional. It is usually the result of an overstretched business manager overlooking some essential factors because they are too busy to address every key point in a service design.

The different skills and experiences of the business and IT sections also need addressing. For example, business managers understand regulatory issues, but IT may not be aware of them or only have a superficial understanding of such constraints.

Poor understanding of the overall design is another concern because the lines of business in almost every enterprise are entirely dependent on IT. All the supporting organisational services, such as payroll, HR, facilities or purchasing, for example, are IT driven. As a consequence, IT is essential in the customer-oriented services in the lines of business (LoB). Information technology is increasingly fundamental to the value proposition in any business.

Business managers spend an enormous amount of time worrying about IT when problems arise and even more time using IT services (comprised usually of one or more IT applications) that gather, process and spit out the information they need.

Any medium or large enterprise can have several LoB. An insurance company, for example, will almost certainly sell property insurance, personal insurance, holiday insurance and many other products and services. Each of these is likely to be an organisational entity or unit. Other units will also exist, including HR, payroll, audit and finance. Even IT is an organisational unit, which can and will be comprised of other units. The LoB and organisational units will all be supported by a combination of specific IT services. This includes IT services that are dependent on one another and IT services that rely on invisible technology, that is they exist only to support the existence and operations of IT.

The purpose of the LoB is to continue to exist and to create money, or to otherwise ensure that the enterprise serves its stated objectives and goals. Generally, specific business purposes are supported by IT services that were designed and built and operated in house, though operational running of IT services has, increasingly, become outsourced.

The purpose of the organisational units is supported by IT services. These are often off-the-shelf products that may exist outside of internal IT operations (payroll is a common example).

Your business transformation drivers impact your business model. The enterprise architecture requires you to think about governance and strategy regarding your information/data, as well as how to improve and operate delivered services. Furthermore, you must maintain the business, data, service and technology perspectives throughout the creation of your operating model (Figure 1.1).

It is crucial for an enterprise to continuously define, develop and improve services that customers want to use (and, of course, pay for). Services are more than ever IT driven and dependent. Complexity lurks beneath every surface. A required service must be fully understood to know if it is truly of value and worthy of investment. And, without an overall business service architecture, it is difficult to picture every nuance.

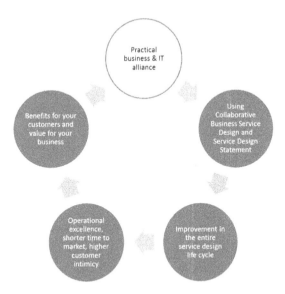

Figure 1.1: Collaborative business service design

Therefore, it is only logical that business stakeholders want to be involved in the development and implementation, or adaptation, of highly IT-driven business services to ensure that different perspectives, interests and principles are included.

1.2 Capturing the characteristics of IT-driven services in a service design statement

Business service design (BSD) is a best practice rooted in design thinking[4] to better understand IT-driven business

---

[4] See for example Stickdorn, M., Schneider, J., editors (2011–2013), This is service design thinking, Basics, tools, cases, Bis

services, its characteristics and requirements, from a business perspective. BSD is rooted in the pragmatic approach and logic of the UK Government Gateway method; the method of service blueprinting and the well-understood stakeholder approach of obtaining executive consensus.

In navigating the BSD approach, you will derive a service design statement **before** you start designing, prototyping and developing. This explains to all the stakeholders what the business wants and needs, what providers should and can deliver, and what essential requirements should be part of the final design and delivery. Using BSD, you will gain improvement in the total service lifecycle, which leads to improved operational excellence, more customer intimacy, faster time to market and more strategic agility.

Publishers, Amsterdam and Polaine, A., Løvlie, L., Reason, B., (2013), service design: From insight to Implementation, Rosenfeld Media. Mootee, I. (2013), Design thinking for strategic innovations; what they can't teach you at business or design school, John Wiley & Sons, New Jersey. Reason, B, Løvlie, L., Brand Flu, M. (2016), Service Design for Business; A practical guide to optimize the customer experience, John Wiley & Sons, Osterwalder, A., Pigneur, Y., Bernarda, G., Smith, A., Smith (2014), New Jersey. Value Proposition Design, how to create products and services customers want, John Wiley & Sons, Hoboken, New Jersey.

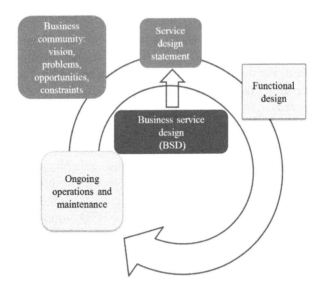

Figure 1.2: Positioning the service design statement

The service design statement (SDS) provides the link between the needs of the business and the detailed functional design needed to start the development or improvement of service offerings. The needs of the business (and what the business will value) are captured in a language of text and pictures, in facts and metaphors and in the business and technical principles. These components will engage all stakeholders (demand and supply alike) in the understanding of the full-service offering.

The BSD approach to deriving a SDS is a practical and powerful tool to help you identify the four essential elements needed to assure your business stakeholders that you can achieve the necessary outcomes. These elements will help you:

1. To promote the coherent design (and possible disaggregation of services) so that fundamental issues and requirements of the requirements are mapped, based on different perspectives between demand and supply.

   When you use the method what will the deliverables be? Examples include:

   - The description and justification of the service.

   - How the service will be delivered (i.e. the interfaces).

   - What customers and users want – quality requirements, useful service level agreements (SLAs) and contracts. You may want to think about the 'c**US**tom**ERS**'. In other words, that a customer and a user might be the same party, or they may be in different organisational groups within the enterprise.

   - What suppliers need – including the functional requirements that can be supported by SLAs and contracts.

2. To obtain insight into the dynamics between stakeholders within an enterprise.

   The financial component is often viewed as the most important, but it does not solely influence the final decision. Board decisions are also made based on other considerations too; this is discussed in Chapter four. Important questions include:

   - How does this decision affect my standing in the enterprise?

- Do I really understand the changes?
- How much certainty is there about the projected outcome?
- What freedom do I have in the longer term to adjust matters?

A certain level of empathy and understanding helps to design service offerings so that they are acceptable for the various stakeholders within the enterprise. Will you always immediately create the best design? Probably not. Because the first draft is never the final picture. It is the start of a development and deployment process and, consequently, the beginning of the discussion.

3. To reflect on and formulate a practical and realistic roadmap.

   Think about the service as a roadmap that provides insight into:

   - Any changes that might need to be developed.
   - How to coordinate progress with the mandated strategic direction and the necessary underlying strategic programmes.
   - The necessary resources and capabilities needed.
   - Specific aspects or issues that arise requiring extra care.
   - Whether you are working as planned.

A roadmap helps you to understand the underlying processes and provide support for discussions with, and the involvement of, the different stakeholders during the development process. The roadmap approach fits well with Agile and DevOps methodologies as you will make quicker progress by prototyping the big picture at an early stage. This is especially true when a service is innovative or has no precedent. It might be impossible to find anyone that can provide experience to the design. As such, we recommend that a solid foundation is in place so you can build on and add features as time progresses.

4. Explore ideas or problems, and think about and develop possible interventions.

The scenarios and possible interventions explicitly create a dialogue between the parties concerned. Information obtained from previous BSD sessions then help to enrich this dialogue. The BSD 'constellation' (discussed later) does provide guidance about decisions to be made, and supports the understanding and exploring of their consequences.

1.3 From business vision to operation: methods to use

ITIL is one of several good practices to ensure that a service operates as expected (there are a myriad of other practices including Service Integration And Management (SIAM) and various ISO standards). In Figure 1.3, we provide an example of how the generic service development model is supported by many frameworks. In advance, we apologise to those who miss the appearance of their favourite framework or standard, but we must get the point across in one picture.

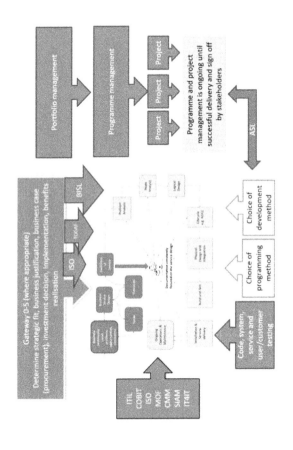

Figure 1.3: Methods and frameworks used to develop IT services

Later, in Figure 2.1, you will be able to see an expanded version of the service lifecycle steps in the centre of the diagram. In the context of the service lifecycle we have placed the well-known methods, not necessarily the one (or more) with which you may be familiar with. And where many choices exist, we have consolidated the listings using project management, PRINCE2 or PMI as examples.

The point of the illustration is that when it comes to the development of business services, there are many methods that will help you manage projects, or systems to help you with your analysis or coding. However, there are not so many to help you design your service effectively in relation to your stakeholders' needs.

1.4 Who should read this guide to fundamentals?

This guide is intended for anyone responsible for designing and implementing IT-driven services, or involved in their operation.

It is designed to help those who want to take examinations and obtain certificates at different experience levels, and covers the essential facts from the ITGP published book *Collaborative Business Design; Improving and innovating the design of IT-driven business services*.

Enterprises with a 'business relationship' role or organisational unit can use this guide to help them identify the most important IT requirements of the business and ensure that these are implemented in any of the solutions proposed by internal or external suppliers.

On the supply side, any internal or external provider of a service, whether IT based or not, will also benefit. Think about your service managers, contract managers, bid managers, lead architects, requirement analysts, etc.

This guide may also prove to be useful to consultants involved with the set up or professionalisation of business service design and to students of business administration, business informatics and service management.

2. UNDERSTANDING IT-DRIVEN SERVICE REQUIREMENTS

Don't ever take a fence down until you know the reason it was put up.

G K Chesterton

2.1 What is a business service?

Think about any airline. BA, United, America, Easy Jet, it doesn't matter. Now, define the service.

Depending on your perspective, this service could be taking people from point A to B. Another person might add the word 'safely'. Someone else might highlight that buying a ticket is part of that service. What about on-board catering? And we have not even started to discuss the services that begin at the airport, including the check in, baggage membership of frequent flyer clubs, etc. And, remember, the enterprise (that is, the owner of the airline) may only be in business to make money, and not necessarily to provide the best service to the passenger.

Now, which of the services we mentioned is a business service and which is IT? The answer is that all are business services that depend on IT and the 'IT services' and organisational units we mentioned in chapter one support the lines of business of the air carrier.

A service can be defined from two perspectives: the demand side and the supply side, although both definitions should match with regards to the different outcomes they produce. Suppliers (providers) will often focus on the development and the maintenance of the output that is asked for. Business (or demand) focuses on attaining the outcome. And all parties anticipate that the output should be predicated on those outcomes. Of course, this is not an easy thing to do but mostly through inattention, providers sometimes forget (or perhaps do not know how) to define services from the perspective of customer needs and responsibility.

All enterprises depend on IT services in their business processes. A random list of enterprise business services demonstrates this:

- Government subsidy for different business sectors (e.g. agriculture, regional economy) – this will involve a large body, maybe more than one, to organise and execute the processes and multiple IT applications to make it all work.
- Pensions and social security payment – imagine all the activities, processes and underlying IT systems needed to pay pensions and social security to those who are entitled.
- Online education (actually, online just about anything) – including portals, registers and all the different business processes, such as registration, distribution, examinations, etc.
- Insurance agreements – including screening and accepting applicants or paying claims to those who are entitled.

Services are enterprise-wide. As a result, we should focus on designing services that fulfil the requirements of any customer in any sector. A final 'definitive' definition of 'services' is therefore hard to find. Thus, we prefer an approach in which we define services as having key characteristics, rather than definitive statements that are open to interpretation:

- Services may not be entirely tangible. For example, an 'office cleaning service'.
- Services comprise of a series of activities. For example, the request and delivery of items that must go through procurement.
- Services are often produced and consumed directly, such as the handling of a request for information or making reservations.
- The customer may (to a greater or lesser extent) participate in the provision of services, such as creating access cards that require a photograph or obtaining photographs for a passport. Another example is that of an office move to a new geographic location.
- The customer participates actively in the service, where services are in fact performed (and manufacturing only takes place) when the customer makes a request. On demand publishing, for example.
- Services are most often not 'pure IT' but more often are heavily IT driven.

Enterprise IT services are supported by the IT infrastructure, which is comprised of hardware, software, and computer-related communications. The technology within IT intensive services may:

- Range from access to a single application (such as a payroll system) to a complex set of facilities including many applications (providing state pensions or social services).

- Be provided from a central system or, as is the case with office automation, could be spread across many hardware and software platforms.

> Defining an IT service that is deployed in support of business services can be controversial.
>
> According to ITIL, the most widely respected framework for managing the IT infrastructure:
>
> 'A service is the provision, operation and maintenance of an (IT) infrastructure, enabling access to information systems, applications and data to the business transaction of a customer, in support of one or more business areas. It may be perceived by the customer of the service as a coherent and self-contained entity.'
>
> The ITIL definition is predicated on the reality that operational running pertains to all business services and ITIL of course focuses on the 'effective running and maintenance of the IT infrastructure'.[5]
>
> In this guide to the fundamentals of collaborative business service design, we focus on a wider definition, which recognises that IT-driven services are defined from a business perspective.

---

[5] ITIL Service Design (2011), 2011 edition, Best Management Practice, Second edition, United Kingdom, Stationery Office.

2.2   Service lifecycle

Life would be simple if designing services happened only in a 'greenfield'. The reality is much harsher. Architectural service design is almost always in a 'brownfield' situation, for example. Many decisions have been made in advance, the market is a given, and you must deal with legacy systems and methods that would be costly, if not impossible, to ignore. Policies are set, people have made their mind up about things that you want to change, but cannot, and IT is as usual, changing everything in sight trying to keep up with the latest digitisation strategies and trends.

We must accept that services have a lifecycle. They exist and eventually they change. Sometimes, they are retired from use altogether. A service lifecycle (Figure 2.1) is a representation of the complete lifetime of a service from initial conception to final decommissioning. Generically, you will find that any lifecycle model does not differ very much from that shown. The major difference in most is what kind of service (business, IT-driven business, IT development or IT infrastructure) is the subject. This figure is the focus for all the hundreds of IT good practices shown in Figure 1.2.

A project lifecycle, which is really all that a service lifecycle claims to be, can be used for planning purposes. It is the sequence of stages through which services pass. The lifecycle covers the following stages:

- The starting point – when the service need is first specified and written.

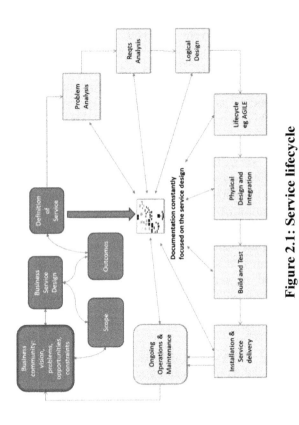

Figure 2.1: Service lifecycle

- The service development lifecycle – the period of time that begins with the decision to develop a service and ends when an acceptable service is delivered for implementation.
- The service implementation.
- The service as part of the operation.
- The decision to renew, improve or decommission the service. In the case of renewal or improvement, the lifecycle starts again with development. In the case of decommissioning, activities must be put in place to phase out the service.

Agile development really means just following these same steps very quickly. A total service design must incorporate all aspects of a service. Thus, a business service using IT will almost certainly involve applications development; an engineered device, a radar installation or car, for example, will involve engineers as well as applications developers. So, a service incorporates lots of building blocks. Each building block has its own lifecycle. For example an application, something 'used' by someone to transact an automated component of an IT intensive business service, is part of the total service that incorporates the ITIL service lifecycle, which focuses on IT supporting services.

2.3 Requirements origin and perspective

An important success factor to obtain the services that you need (but did not necessarily ask for) is getting the requirements right. This is not as easy as one might think. Somehow, there is a gap between the wants and needs of the business and the offerings suppliers provide.

So, why is it so difficult to get the requirements right? What are the pertinent questions a business should ask their provider of their IT services to get things right? How does the business get a grip on IT development in relation to the IT-driven business processes?

When it comes to designing IT intensive business services and models, approaches are few and far between. To obtain better insight, to correct for prejudices and miscommunications of the necessary requirements, and to get a better grip on IT development, we need to understand all the differing requirements of the different stakeholders and balance these in an optimal design that is fit for use. We used existing best practices to build the approach that we have called business service design. This approach favours:

- A structured working method that improves categorisations and retrieval of essential issues and requirements, and decreases complexity (leading to improved clarity).
- Simultaneously combining analysis and converging perspectives.
- Eliminating error by documenting results.
- Involving all essential stakeholders and their perspectives/concerns.

How do we obtain the correct requirements for your IT-intensive service offering and where do they come from? Well, they arise from **all** the different stakeholders that have a stake in the service offering. We explicitly state **all** the stakeholders because we think requirements should come from demand *and* supply

Of course, it is not the intention for all stakeholders to necessarily agree. Sometimes, requirements cannot be matched because of non-existent technology, or because the costs are too high. What is important is that all stakeholders agree on the service offering that will be designed. And not only from the demand side, the supplier side must also agree because the design must be attainable within the parameters set by the customer.

We distinguish between different sets or groups of requirements in Figure 2.2.

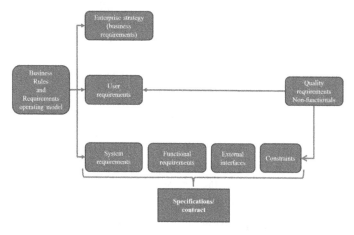

Figure 2.2: The requirement roadmap

Strategic business requirements comprise business requirements and business rules. Business requirements define objectives and strategies that define the mission and vision of the enterprise. For example, accountability and responsibilities, specific policies about privacy or other restrictions brought about by corporate governance policies.

Within operational requirements one can distinguish functional requirements, system requirements, external interfaces and technical constraints.

- Functional requirements – specify the behaviour of the service and the functions of the services. For example, how it records, computes, transforms or transmits data.
- System requirements – describe the requirements for a service that is composed of multiple parts (systems or other services, such as IT services).
- External interfaces – define and describe the interactions with various other resources, such as services or systems that are (or must be) in place.
- Technical constraints – describe constraints that originate through technology choices (or constraints), policy demands, legislation etc.

There is then a dramatic difference between business rules design and operational/functional design. Operational personnel will need to know (IT) functionality. The business will also want to be assured that accurate processing will take place. However, their primary focus is on the outcome of the information being processed.

The business though cannot abrogate responsibility for technology decisions to the supplier. For example, if a file sharing utility is needed and the decision is entirely at the discretion of the supplier then something (such as Dropbox or a similar offering) might be the proposed technology solution. But the supplier might be completely unaware that corporate policy forbids the use of commercial external platforms.

2.4 Business service design

Business Service Design (BSD) is built on practical principles and best practices. The basic assumptions of BSD are that:

- The target formulated by the customer ('the business outcome') becomes 'a beacon' for all parties involved in the design throughout the design process.
- There is an owner of the service design offering who feels responsible for the entire quality and effectiveness of the service lifecycle.
- Exploration and design with input from every relevant discipline is possible, including the customer, financial controller, users, CIO or deputy CIO, CIO adviser, strategist, IT management consultant, business consultant, information analyst, IT architect, owner of the service, service manager, programme manager, sourcing manager, purchasing, contract manager, service level manager, account manager. If necessary, even the company cat!
- A service, a system or an application is not simply the design result. The result is a total set of requirements of the desired service (including the business requirements, user requirements, demand-side and customer requirements, and functional and system requirements).

BSD merges the pragmatism and logic of the UK Government Gateway method, which is the method of service blueprinting and that of the stakeholder approach to gaining consensus. This includes the:

- Gateway method – The Gateway process defines review gates, or points throughout the lifecycle of acquisition and/or implementation of products and/or services. Gateways are undertaken for all levels of procurement projects, as defined by the project profile model. Requests for Gateway reviews are initiated by senior responsible owners/project owners.[6]

- Service blueprinting: This is a customer focused approach for service innovation and service improvement. A service blueprint allows an enterprise to explore all the issues inherent in creating or managing a service. The service processes are visualised, points of contact and accompanying actions and processes are identified, and their relationships, are made explicit.[7]

- Stakeholder approach: This approach emphasises that the exploration of the enterprise need must arise from two perspectives: those of the stakeholders in the enterprise and those of managers of IT and networks. The stakeholder approach emphasises the importance of investing in relationships with those who have an interest in the stability of these relationships. These stakeholders are organisational units or individuals within the enterprise or, in the environment of the enterprise, whose decisions impact the way the enterprise is operated and managed. Of course, these stakeholders are impacted by the goals of the

---

[6] See OCG Gateway, Bureau Gateway, Ministerie van Binnenlandse Zaken en Koninkrijksrelaties and Major Projects Authority (MPA) UK Government.

[7] See Shostack, G.L. (1984), Designing services that deliver, Harvard Business Review, January–february 1984, pp. 133–139.

enterprise. The relations between them are characterised by simultaneous cooperation and competition. In other words, sometimes a stakeholder domain will demand independence from a recommended course of action, such as choosing between solutions. The interdependence between the parties is evident.[8]

The BSD approach comprises four phases, initially surfacing need and service demand by identifying the senior responsible owner and secondly, the desired outcome of the service offering. The third phase is the analysis and synthesis using 'the service constellation' that is central in gathering the service design requirements then, the fourth phase, setting out the description of the final service design offering.

In following the BSD approach, you can work through the four phases using the canvas in Figure 2.3.

1. The senior responsible owner (SRO, a role title found in PRINCE2) is identified and the desired service offering is established. Most likely, this will be the role of the program manager for the service design.

---

[8] See Freeman, R.E. (2010), Strategic Management, a stakeholder approach, first printing 1984, digital printed 2010. Cambridge University Press. Mastenbroek, W.F.G. (2005), Conflicthantering en organisatie-ontwikkeling. Proefschrift Leiden, vierde herziene druk, Samsom.

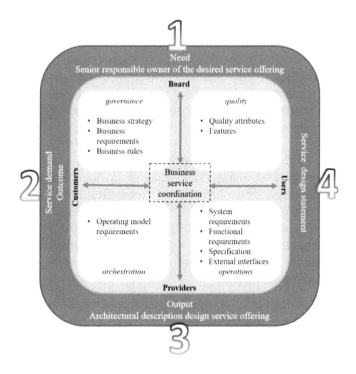

Figure 2.3: Business service design approach

2. It must be clear what the outcome should be. To begin with, you need to have a solid understanding about the service outcomes and output.

3. At the heart of the BSD, there is the service constellation that supports the essential analysis and synthesis of the service offering requirements. The analysis and synthesis go through cycles. Steps in a cycle are:

   a. Establishing stakeholders and their need or responsibility

b.   Understanding service transactions
c.   Understanding needed resources, risks and compliance
d.   Choosing instruments for agreement. Finally, the output is translated into the SDS. After the analysis and synthesis, using the service constellation described in section 2.3.3, there are a number of steps you must take before you can compose the elements of the service design into the SDS.

2.4.1   Need and senior responsible owner

The SRO should have a position at the Board/GM level and must be responsible for the commission of a Gateway review of a major project, a survey or a feasibility study, or a complete service design. In this way, we can position the BSD as the overall business architectural transaction.

Someone within the enterprise is responsible for service offering delivery. Depending on the size and type of enterprise, who (manager or team) or what (department or several organisational units), the responsibility will be defined differently. This responsibility is often called service offering management (SOM).[9] SOM focuses on the customer and the type of product and/or services they need. Activities that SOM oversees are:

- customer base and need
- service offering
- creation and delivering needed services

---

[9] Tillman, G. (2008), The business oriented CIO; A guide to market-driven management, John Wiley & Sons, Hoboken, New Jersey.

- performance management.

To understand the dynamics of the SOM, the enterprise is explored from two perspectives: the perspective of the stakeholders of the service offering and that of management of the enterprise and networks in general, and service delivery specifically.

Stakeholders will be identified from the perspective of those who are responsible that services come to fruition (or even come to an end as we see later) and are maintained. Stakeholders differ in every enterprise and in every service, that you would like to design.

Often a senior responsible service owner has many questions:

- Is this service the one I really need?
- Does the service fit my required outcomes?
- Should I invest in it?
- Can I minimise risks?
- How to involve all the essential stakeholders?
- Will the service add value?
- Can we control costs involved?
- What are the costs?
- and a hundred more...

As you can see most thoughts often do not focus on the 'how' of the service but on the impact and the consequences the service has in the larger scheme of things.

2.4.2 Business service coordination: I think therefore I am

For analysis and understanding purposes, and for the purposes of the BSD, it is necessary to identify someone that takes this delegated role and overall responsibility. This entity is the business service coordination (BSC) role. The BSC can be an individual or an organisational unit in the enterprise and in some cases even a virtual role.

Often the representative of the SRO is positioned in an organisational entity, which also takes decisions about sourcing and managing business information. Often, this role is created when the enterprise has outsourced functions (most frequently IT) and needs to retain knowledge to manage suppliers effectively. In the UK, this is often known as the intelligent customer function. Sometimes, this 'intelligent customer' function is called the retained organisation and the design of business services using IT can be part of it.

In many enterprises, you will find that there is no direct relationship between the different stakeholders. Often, a responsible function or agent is placed between the main stakeholders. It is impossible to identify all the specific characteristics of the responsible functions or agents without sound knowledge of the enterprise. BSD is an approach that assists with recognising the requirements and, if necessary, delegating appropriate responsibilities to a business service coordinator, or coordination team/role, so that an architectural service design can be qualified. And afterwards, the BSC role ensures that requirements are allocated to the appropriate roles in the enterprise so that the transactions are met.

2.4.3 Outcome and output must dictate behaviour

The direction of an enterprise, as put down in the mission and vision, answers questions, such as, 'Where is this going? What business are we in? What business should we be in?'. The strategic directions are beacons to the development and design of business services. We must differentiate between output and outcome. The outcome is the focus of the mission and vision and should be the umbrella of all outputs that result from the different actions in the enterprise.

Output and outcome are not only 'What you get', they should be 'What you expected and what you asked for'. This, of course, takes us back to warranty and fitness for purpose. Too often, the desired outcome is not fully articulated and all parties run off to their happy places and either wait for Christmas to happen, or start coding the reindeer before thinking about what Santa is going to put on the sledge.

> Examples of questions to ask:
> - What is the scope of the services?
> - Where is the service/output delivered?
> - When is the service/output delivered?
> - Is the intended result(s) fully understood (output)?
> - Is this service dependent upon other services?
> - When does this service contribute to the mandated/desired output?
> - When does this service contribute to the mandated/desired outcome?

> - What additional factors can influence the success of this service?

It must be clear to all stakeholders what desired outcome and output should be. A clear description of output and outcome in the architectural service design process is imperative.

2.4.4   Service constellation

The stakeholder approach that is the basis of BSD thinking will help the SRO to understand the specifications of the new or adapted business services in relation to the conditions or opportunities. A Stakeholder is any group or individual who can affect, or is impacted by, the achievement of the purpose of the enterprise.

BSD focuses on the creation and delivery of business service. Hence the canvas in figure 2.3, which is called service constellation, must focus on the four essential groups that make this happen: board, customers, providers and users. Of course, behind and next to these four groups many more are trying to influence the process, output and outcome. So you make sure as Business Service Coordinator the SRO understands the central tensions and forces corresponding to the optimal business service.

Why do we call our image of the stakeholders and their perspectives the service constellation? To us it is similar to the night sky: there are patterns that people can see because they are told they exist (The Plough, Orion's Belt) and there are some that you just cannot see no matter what you are told, and there are some you find for yourself.

The purpose of the service constellation is to ensure that the service deployed is the one that was desired, and that any design constraint issues (cost, perhaps, or security) were fully explored and understood before everyone signed up to development.

In the third step of BSD, you must navigate the service design constellation to establish service requirements. Seeing our service constellation for the first time can be mind boggling. It comprises many different elements that, when aggregated, help you to understand all the requirements that make up a service offering.

2.4.5 Service design statement

The result of your initial labours is the SDS, or service design statement. That is, a description of the IT intensive business services that you will take forward into the development of one or more services. After navigating the service constellation, you should have gathered all the information needed. Success depends on whether all the information is available to cover all the information in the design and development stages. From a business point of view, you must have all the business information needs to justify further investment and sign off.

Service constellation thinking facilitates extensively checking the service design offering and governing the full-service requirement. From a supplier perspective, you should probably work out some more details to complete the design stage and make the service offering feasible. However, the approach will uncover enough information in the design stage to influence design choices made and understand the capabilities needed. Therefore, at this phase we prefer to describe the output as a *description* of a service offering, rather than the design of the service offering.

BSC is the link for the enterprise with their customers and the providers of services. The objective of BSC is effective control of results of (insourced and outsourced) services by controlling demand as well as supply. For architectural service design and exploration, the BSC is the delegated service owner and the position where control will be managed. Figure 2.4 illustrates (in the centre) the most likely functions that will be undertaken and the complexity of the overall environment. The BSC can never take over the responsibility of the customer. However, their responsibility is delivering what is needed. The customer has final responsibility for ensuring that what is needed is fit for purpose.

Figure 2.4: The central role of the BSC

2.5   The Business Service Design session

A BSD session generally comprises four phases: intake, preparation, analysis and synthesis and conclusion. Table 2.1 explains the different phases. Depending on the complexity of the service design you will find that the different phases take longer or more stakeholders need to participate. A golden rule does not exist. It depends on you as the leading practitioner, your experience and circumstances such as existing constraints. A constraint may be money (or lack of it), existing capabilities, perhaps even ambition.

Table 2.1: Four phases in a Business Service Design session

Phases	1. Intake	2. Preparation	3. Analysis and synthesis	4. Conclusion
Goal	Intake Determination whether BSD can assist	Initial meetings Logistics Communication	Using BSD to discover the desired service design	Accepted design description and design repository and clearance for next step
Activities	Setting outcome Intake and request Selecting and inviting stakeholders Budget plan	Time table Program Location Budget available	Insight in output and outcome in relation to business strategy Insight in coherent service Insight in requirements Insight in roadmap	Service description Service design document Service design repository

Phases	1. Intake	2. Preparation	3. Analysis and synthesis	4. Conclusion
			Insight in risks and compliance Insight in needed agreement	
Action Responsible Service Owner	Explaining needed outcome in relation to business strategy Agreeing on budget to design service	None	Being available for additional information or communication new relevant information	Acceptance and sign off
Action Project Manager for Service Design (PM-SD)	Setting up service design programme	Bringing all stakeholders together	Final responsibility that design is made.	Making the delivery Evaluation Lessons to be learned

A graphical representation of the four phases is illustrated in Figure 2.5. Some people like words, some people like pictures. Whatever your preference, just be sure you cover everything!

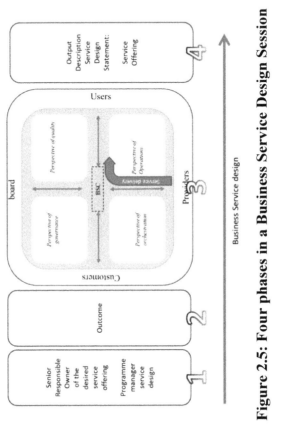

Figure 2.5: Four phases in a Business Service Design Session

In the next chapter, we will begin by explaining the needs of the stakeholders and their dynamics.

3. STAKEHOLDER DYNAMICS IN THE SERVICE CONSTELLATION

One doesn't discover new lands without consenting to lose sight of the shore for a very long time. Andre Gide

3.1 Delivering what is needed: Business service design

The enterprise focuses on outcome. There is a need or responsibility to accomplish something. For example, 'ensure trains run on time', 'make sure social security and pensions are paid', 'be sure a new generation workspace is installed and functioning', 'make sure that salaries are paid'. It is not merely the working of the application that is the heart of service development. Services must support desired outcomes; they must be designed to make sure that *the salary application* is in place to ensure salaries are paid. Furthermore, good design should ensure that all other activities that support employees have been considered. For example, access to information through a tablet or smartphone, or ensuring that people have access to all their information, anytime, anywhere, anyplace.

Customers often do not want the service they think they asked for, they need something else that perhaps they were not adept at explaining. Therefore, it is of utmost importance to delve deeper into the necessary outcome than the requested output (a service or contract that looks right but does not stand up to usage in operation, for example). Most likely they need some other 'thing' that helps them reach their outcome.

This should lead to three specific actions. First, to design and develop the service offering you must account for the different perspectives within the enterprise and between demand and supply, and try to understand what is really needed. You must have insight into the service offering. Second, you need to have insight into the elements that will comprise the service offering. And third, when preparing for design of the service, describing the position of the needed services in the service lifecycle (is it completely new, is it a major change, is it an IT service, does it require applications to be developed). This step is essential to understand the right transactions.

To gain the essential requirements, we developed Business Service Design (BSD). At the core of BSD is the service constellation, as depicted in Figure 3.1. In this chapter and the next, we will explore the different elements of the service constellation and explain how it helps you to compose the total set of service requirements.

The service constellation is defined by the stakeholder participants (the actors) and the requirements generated between these actors because of how they interact. As mentioned in Chapter two, the central actor is BSC, the representative of the owner of the service. The relationships arise between domains because of stakeholder interactions and dependencies. Each domain defines specific requirements that are particular to the stakeholders involved, as can be seen in Figure 3.1.

In this chapter, we specifically focus on the dynamics and the underlying activities that make up the relationships between the stakeholders. These relationships will materialise in transactions that are part of the service offering. Transactions follow on from capabilities and resources that are deployed and serve to make agreements between stakeholders.

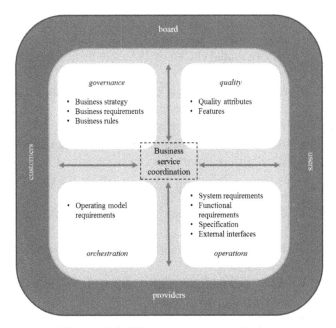

Figure 3.1: The service constellation

3.2   A stakeholder view of the enterprise

There are four stakeholder elements or strands. Think of them as DNA components from which a myriad of combinations will create different outputs (and outcomes). All the strands are of equal importance; it is how they are combined in different ways that ensure the correct output. We could argue that combining the strands incorrectly is, in biological terms, the same as a mutation in what was really the intention of nature.

Examples of questions to ask:

- Who are the stakeholders (middle management, major users, departments e.g. sales, finance, service managers, etc.)? What are their needs and responsibilities?
- How do I relate their needs and responsibility to the needed service output/outcome?
- Who are the decision makers?
- What type of users/employees/citizens are there?
- What different job roles can be identified?
- Is there a difference for users whom are visually impaired? Or deaf? Or disabled?
- Who will pay for the service or who will make budget available?
- What are the customer/user/general management expectations?
- Who are the providers, are they internal or external or a combination?
- What are the provider's expectations?
- What are the expectations of users, customers, providers and general management (board)?
- Is the strategy to which this service is contributing approved by the stakeholders?
- Is the service matched to general enterprise policy, and have stakeholders approved?

> - Is stakeholder expertise present or available to deliver this service?
> - How are the stakeholders involved in this service?

3.2.1 Stakeholders from the business services coordination perspective

Although there are many stakeholders within an enterprise, to produce meaningful services that are purchased and consumed by users, BSC focuses on the four main stakeholders. These are the board, customers, providers and users. Each has dominion over a specific domain of the enterprise.

The different stakeholders make up four domains within the service constellation. A domain is the area of the enterprise that is specific to a stakeholder or group of stakeholders (and, of course, a domain will most often represent many individuals within an enterprise).

Within each domain environment are several measures that can be deployed to calibrate and monitor the dynamic equilibrium. There are four different domains:

1. operations/operational services (delivery)
2. orchestration (tactical services)
3. governance (strategic services)
4. quality (experience and features).

Examples of typical questions and consequent requirements that are asked in the different domains are presented in Figure 3.2.

Demand is driven by the board, users and customers. Effectively, there is a balance between supply and demand thus, architectural service design is a tension between the five roles (don't forget the BSC!) and these four surrounding domains.

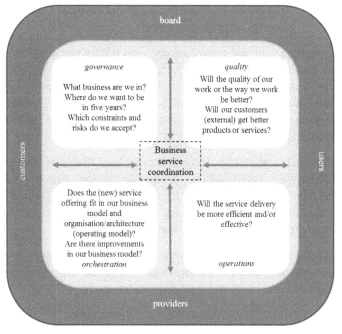

**Figure 3.2: Typical questions within
the different domains**

3.2.2   Users

In explaining the different roles and responsibilities of the stakeholders, we first start with users. Users consume the services and products from the suppliers. In Figure 3.3, we provide just a few examples of the roles you might need (and, in some cases, will need) in the enterprise. Some of these are advisory, some external. Some of the roles are guardian roles; can you identify what you need?

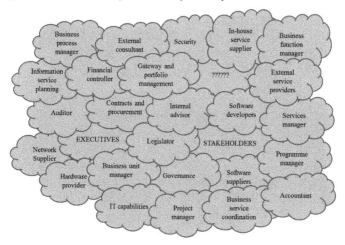

Figure 3.3: Roles that exist in the enterprise

In general, users do not pay for their internal services. In market situations, you will find that users might contribute by paying for products that are delivered. But after that it is not their decision about which products are to be built, nor can they influence quality levels and quantities. For example, when a passport is needed, civilians must pay but have no influence on the quality of the product or service. If we don't like the product (or service) we can complain, though the chances of influencing any change are minimal. Try calling Microsoft and asking for a change in PowerPoint.

3.2.3   Providers

At the base of Figure 3.1, you will see that providers (whether they are internal or external suppliers) deliver the actual service and technology to users who need them to get their work done or their wishes fulfilled. The service might be provided to users in accordance with a product and service catalogue and maintained, for example, through service management and a service desk.

3.2.4   Customers

The customer acts within the boundaries set by the Board. Often, customers are viewed as those who have the mandate and budget to carry out strategies to realise the enterprise's vision. The most important customer is also, generally, on the management board or in control of management of the portfolio for business operations. Effectively, they pay for generic or basic services.

Thus, services are purchased for users by customers, so they can perform the necessary work efficiently and accurately. Based on the needs of the users, a budget is agreed alongside a price to be paid to provide the services. The specific needs of users are often laid down in internal service level agreements (SLAs); where services are procured from outside of the enterprise and the agreements most often relate to an overall contract. Users must accept the SLAs made with these third parties.

It may be that the basic service for some customer groups is not appropriate or insufficient for their needs. In that case, these customers can, through the governance organisation, negotiate separate agreements on additional services and different service levels. Additionally, for alternative arrangements, the board can decide whether to pass on additional costs. These specific arrangements are often referred to as having been designated to specific budgets.

3.2.5 Board of directors/general management

General management has overall responsibility for the performance of the enterprise. They discuss and decide upon the mission and vision of the enterprise. Focus is on the business model, market, profit and loss, and return on investment. They establish leadership and guiding principles and set policy on the operation and development of the organisation.

3.2.6 Business service coordination (BSC)

It is up to BSC to balance sometimes divergent interests of supply and demand in such a way that everyone can be satisfied. If the emphasis is solely on cost, suppliers will eventually become frustrated, inclining them to reduce cost at the expense of quality.

The needs of the internal customer and users are recognised in different ways. BSC is aware of the market and the current and future needs of the enterprise, and can advise effectively for decision makers. It is assumed that there are effective arrangements with the service providers. A total budget is, therefore, identified at the outset. If the total budget is insufficient, or providers are an issue, then this is explored in the process.

BSC outlines the need, and translates these functional requirements into a technical package of requirements that reflect the market supply. In addition, the outline considers demands from the environment in which the enterprise operates, such as architectural standards, branding, strategic principles, and so on. In addition, BSC will also advise the board on matters, such as new developments, standardisation policy and cost.

Based on the user experience, measurements (e.g. audits, satisfaction surveys, panels, etc.), and the performance of contracts, BSC obtains an idea of the perceived quality of the services being operated. The results are reported back to general management and the board. At this time, BSC may take the initiative to advise about new developments (motivated by the users or service providers).

BSC, therefore, takes a role in the creation and implementation of policy and strategy. IT oversees the invocation of policy advice to the strategic goals and directs the adoption to strategic plans (security, housing plan, subcontracting plan, etc.).

A clear relationship is also needed between the BSC roles and enterprise use of Gateway methods, and programme and project office roles and methods. In some enterprises, the roles might well all be in one place (or held by one person) because the stakeholders are easy to identify, and the size of the organisation is relatively small. In larger enterprises with multiple organisation units and lines of business, it would be unwise to expect one person, or one group, to be able to juggle multiple perspectives.

3.3   The domains

The five stakeholders exist in four different domains (or in some instances 'kingdoms', in worse scenarios, 'fiefdoms') in the service constellation, as shown in Figure 3.4. These are:

1. the domain of operations (or delivery)
2. the domain of orchestration
3. the domain of governance
4. the domain of quality.

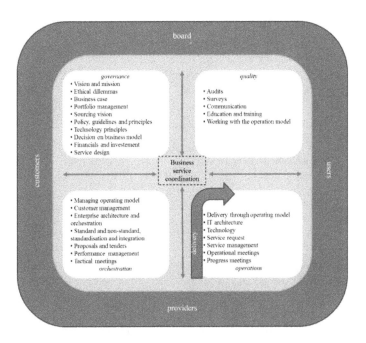

Figure 3.4: The management domains

The domain sets out the activities that arise between the different stakeholders.

3.3.1 Domain: Operations

In this domain, the relationships between users, suppliers and the BSC are maintained, with the focus on the actual delivery of services. This applies also to the actual implementation of agreed projects and changes for which tenders have been issued. That means that the delivered products and services are known and recorded in a definitive list, or portfolio of products and services.

Typical questions asked in the domain operations

How can we improve on our delivery?
What service levels are relevant?
Why are our users unhappy?
How are we in control of our operations?
Does our helpdesk cover all requests?
Why does no one like me?

3.3.2 Domain: Quality

The quality domain is formed by the relationships BSC maintains with users and the board. The quality of service is a result of the agreements made by BSC with customers and suppliers, and the method of delivery. General management, or the board, is largely preoccupied (after making money), mainly with enabling employees to be able to continuously and smoothly conduct their work (which the cynical among us would say is making it easier to make money).

Tension will arise because users are not directly confronted with the costs. Therefore, users will be more inclined to overstate their needs and requirements, especially in times of cost rationalisation. This will increase the discrepancy between 'wants and needs' and available options. Value should be a key consideration; warranty and fitness for purpose must be considered but customers may not fully understand what users need in these terms. This situation is difficult to influence directly.

First, BSC can make sure that the service suppliers are performing well; second, BSC can regularly assess customer satisfaction through surveys or panels. Third, they can offer training and, finally, BSC can actively involve customers in pilot or innovative developments. Quality can be addressed in many dimensions, including enterprise policy regarding standards (software quality, security, operational management or perhaps governance) and promotion of good practice frameworks, such as BiSL next, PRINCE2 or ITIL.

Typical questions asked in the domain of quality

- What is the 'U-X', the customer experience?
- Who are our 'ambassadors'?
- What is the intended result of a new service?
- What do major consumers of the service want and need?
- Do we have access to all relevant information?
- What are the key characteristics of behaviour and culture?
- When doing the right things right, will it matter?

3.3.3 Domain: Governance

The domain formed by the relationships between BSC, its customers and general management, is regarded as governance. The content of the work in this area is generally strategic. It concerns the agreements resulting from enterprise goals, legal frameworks and financial areas, and which roles are required for the direction (advisory, informative or steering) of the development of long-term services. It can result in exploring or validating the business case. Think of architecture agreements and sourcing policies, portfolio management and policy objectives.

Typical questions asked in the domain of governance

- What is our long range strategic planning? Is it effective?
- What is our value proposition?
- What does management find important in the course/ direction of our enterprise?
- Is our competitive strategy based on our market position?
- What is our competitive advantage?

3.3.4 Domain: Orchestration

When the executive board decides on the foundation for execution, it will be in the domain of orchestration where the operating model is managed and guarded. An operating model is the necessary level of business processes integration and standardisation for delivering goods and services to the users. [10] This domain includes the organisational methods, systems and procedures that dictate the working patterns and formal behaviour of the organisation.

Typical questions asked in the domain of orchestration

- What methods are used?
- What is our operational model?
- How is our financial cycle organised?
- What do competitors do?
- What strategies are in place to realise our vision, do they achieve results?
- What are our capabilities?
- Do we do the right things, right?

In this domain, the relationships between customers and suppliers are maintained. These relationships are reflected in the agreements made between functional needs and the supply of products and services based on price, time and quality. This means that BSC identifies the current and future need, and verifies that the requirements have been translated into agreements with the suppliers. This is done with the support of the procurement and/or purchasing departments.

In the next chapter, we focus on the analysis of the service constellation.

---

[10] See Ross, J., Weill, P, Robertson, S.C. (2006), Enterprise Architecture as strategy; creating a foundation for business execution, Boston MA, Harvard Business School Press.

4. CAPABILITIES AND RESOURCES WITHIN THE CONSTELLATION

Get your facts first, and then you can distort them as much as you please.

Mark Twain

4.1 Transactions, communications, resources and agreements

Stakeholders can and will affect, (and in turn are affected by), the achievements of organisational units. They affect the outcome by communicating, making choices, taking actions, etc. Some of these actions lead to specific transactions (think 'requirements') that are part of the germination of the services and, therefore, should be part of the architectural service design. It is very important that stakeholders communicate at the outset of designing services so that all essential requirements can be gathered.

Within BSD, we make these requirements and accompanying transactions explicit by analysing each domain in the service constellation, finding the essential transactions, extracting data and understanding the necessary resources, risks involved and constraints that are or should be in place. Only then can we be sure of the minimum set of requirements that should be part of the final design. The sum of all the transactions makes up the service offering.

BSD encourages communication. It will only be through communication between the stakeholders that demand or need for specific transactions originates and is managed.

For a transaction between stakeholders to occur, there needs to be a trigger. For example, the questions:

- Are we going to do everything ourselves or are we contracting outside providers? (In other words, does anyone have a clue if we have a sourcing strategy?)
- How can people apply for social security?
- How can we deliver a physical or virtual portal to interface with the users?
- How do we make sure that providers come up with the right solutions that fit our already chosen platform, etc.?

Communications between stakeholders are triggers designed to elicit and deliver transactions or set conditions. Always consider the U-X, the customer experience, when thinking about transactions; what will they be expecting?

To understand what we mean by a transaction, here is a very simple explanation:

- a stakeholder says 'I want wine'
- the supplier stakeholder replies 'No worries, here is some wine'
- or 'What type of wine do you want'
- or 'Do you prefer dry or sweet, more wood taste or fruit?'
- or 'Depends on what you want to spend'
- or even 'No chance, we do not offer alcohol'
- or 'You can only drink wine we buy from Africa'
- or 'You can only order wine that is on card'.

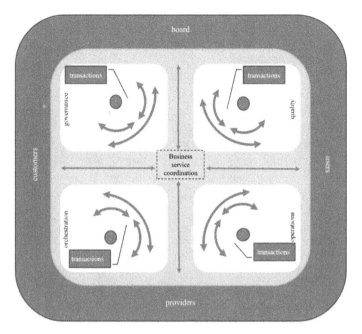

**Figure 4.1: Transactions between stakeholders:
communications that matter to service offering**

You get the idea. When it comes to transactions between external (and internal) suppliers at the operational level, it is generally a more concrete statement of need. When it is a customer (board) request it is more ambiguous. Within BSD, all these requests/requirements are examined one by one, and defined as a 'transaction'.

Here are two examples:

- Providers can ask FOR information or for an action to be undertaken by the user, and users will deliver by providing the information, or taking appropriate action; perhaps business operations need to be suspended before the supplier can make an essential security upgrade.

• Users request a minimum level of working conditions and the board will mandate a standard based on performance indicators. Or users set minimum requirements on working space standards (for example, more than one computer terminal will be needed for each user, necessitating bigger desks). If the Board does not accept the conditions, users will find other jobs or, depending on their levels of patience, inform the Board that work is not possible because everyone is sitting in the lap of another person.

Transactions have several attributes:

4.1.1 Transactions offer something or request something

Communication between stakeholders in a domain leads to questions or offerings. A stakeholder can request portal functionality or can request a budget. A stakeholder can offer policy or strategy on security, or a stakeholder can offer authentication when subscribing to a service.

4.1.2 Transactions have different characteristics

In each domain, there are transactions that come from different requests and deliveries by stakeholders. There are three types of transactions possible between stakeholders and BSC:

1. Physical transactions, for example, those resulting in requirements for applications, platforms, etc.

2. Information transactions, such as guidelines, standards, procedures, information, etc.
3. Relational transactions, for example meetings, conferences, etc. set up to build trust, understanding and reconciliation.

4.1.3   Transactions that are desirable or mandatory

Occasionally, it is not clear whether a need is in fact something that **is** essential. In exploring all the transactions, it will be necessary to conclude whether a transaction is simply desirable or essential to the service delivery.

4.1.4   Transactions set a condition or a delivery

Mandatory or desirable attributes of a transaction can set a condition or lead to a different manner of delivery in each domain. Most physical transactions can be found in the operational domain (e.g. give everyone an iPhone), whereas in the other domains most transactions are for information purposes (e.g. where possible ISO standards should be used to govern building new IT services) and set conditions.

A transaction must be completed for every requirement; if the transaction is not feasible, it must be explicitly rejected, and the impact assessed, noted and reported. A transaction essentially then becomes one of the requirements, either new, or changing something that might already exist. Transactions passed between stakeholder groups (e.g. from a customer to a supplier) require a response to be passed back so that the value of the response can be assessed. All transactions have equal value because each is a requirement. The value of each transaction is perceived differently by the stakeholder groups. If any of the requirements cannot be met, either the requirement is unclear, it is ambiguous, it is unrealistic, or it has risks too great to mitigate.

The transaction groups are board to customer, customer to supplier, users to suppliers and users to the board (and *vice versa*, see Figure 4.1).

Reciprocal is the key word when it comes to transactions. We want to emphasise that transactions can be about provision of a service or product, or transactions can be requests for information. Transactions in the quality, governance and demand domain most often set conditions and therefore can lead to dependencies, opportunities, restrictions, mandatory relationships and connections, etc. These conditions can lead to additional provision, for example the wish that a financial service should be Cloud based will result in additional measures to be put in place before the provider can deliver the financial service to the user. You should gather from this example why we posit that business information decisions cannot be separated from technology decisions.

Consider the complexity of the environment when thinking about stakeholder needs and how they must be balanced with delivery of appropriate services. See the following table for examples of transactions in each domain.

Domain	Example transactions
Governance	Adjusting/creating portfolio management Formulating/sourcing strategy, ecosystem strategy Setting up architectural principles Defining policies, services and organisational units for example on information security, procurement mandate Structural meeting with management, experts, BSC, on architecture, strategy and sourcing Compliance Making investment plans
Quality	Execute audits Satisfaction, satisfaction surveys Establish communication Formulating management by exception Periodical meetings with opinion leaders and heavy users about quality of current and future service offerings and support Planning training programmes Executing road shows, instructions Setting up involvement in pilots and developments
Orchestration	Instantiate relationship management Present product & service catalogue Provide orchestration platform Contracts and service level agreements Managing eco-system Define and issue standards/levels of service/customisation Instantiate tendering processes and project and programme management Procedures, management and organisation Execute performance management

Domain	Example transactions
	Set tactical meetings (incl. contract board)
Operations	Receive calls, portal, desks
	Physical workflows and work instructions
	Account management and instructions
	Operational meetings
	Progress meetings
	Procedures for actual delivery
	Service management
	Service delivery
	Operation system integration

4.2   Customer journey

Transactions are the building blocks of the service blueprint. Ideally, in a service offering all requirements within each domain should match with the requirements made by the stakeholders. Also, we can conclude, as explained, that operation leads to delivery. Delivery (and therefore use) triggers users to assess quality. Ideally, 'experienced' quality should fit the mandated levels of quality and establish trust with operations (we realise this **is** a very idealistic situation). For each domain, we must establish the right requirements and, therefore, the right transaction that adds value to the final holistic service offering.

Each transaction can be positioned in the service offering depending on the transaction type, or its visibility to users, or the influence it has on the delivery to users. We use the technique known as 'blueprinting' to order the different transactions and create their relationships.

The 'core' of your service design offering is the actual delivery (actions leading to service delivery).

However, the requirements influencing the final delivery in each domain result from quality, governance and orchestration requirements. Thus, these are actions that set conditions. See Figure 4.2.

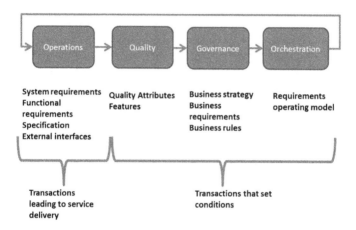

Figure 4.2: Flow of transactions that lead to the desired service offering.

The summation of **all** the essential transactions makes up the service offering.

When do you know you have enough transactions? By using the service blueprinting method to build up the service delivery and its conditions, you will find that

> *there is a point where you will be satisfied because there are diminishing returns on the discussion points. At that time, no further analysis is beneficial. What remains is a last check, which we will explain in section 5.3.*

To build the service design within the constellation, an approach is adapted that first was proposed by G. Lynn Shostack and later explored by others. It will help you structure, design and align transactions as they unfold over time. A standard service blueprint approach does not exist, but there is agreement on two aspects that are always clarified: the user journey over time and the main activities and processes in a service design process.

Use the generic service delivery process to analyse a request. A request is made to the front office that, in cooperation with the back office, leads to service delivery. Service delivery is of course being developed with output in mind. Between the three, there are interactions that must be explored to understand what interfaces will be needed (portal, desk, agent, automated procedure, etc.).[11] A certain part of the service delivery will be visible to users that

---

[11] Practical insight into the service delivery chain based on the front office-back office model and more in depth discussion on the interface between customer and provider can be found in Rouw, L.P. (2015), De service desk; spin in het facilitaire web, tweede herziene druk, VakmediaNet, Aplhen aan den Rijn en Rayport, J.F. & Jaworski, B.J. (2005). Best Face Forward: Why Companies Must Improve their Service Interfaces with Customers. Boston, MA: Harvard Business School Press.

make a request for a particular service. In the blueprint method this is called the 'line of visibility'.

In Figure 4.3 we show the blueprint template.

On the vertical axis, the time line, or more specifically; the customer journey, is plotted. Services have different stages: awareness (a call to action), the start of the action and a road (often rocky!) to reaching the goals and, then, return to business as usual. Thus, in many respects they are like stories.

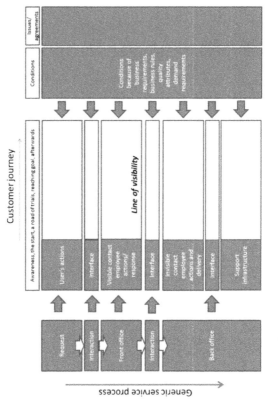

Figure 4.3: Service blueprint template in business service design

This provides a simple framework that helps the participants structure the user journey and experiences, and helps them to understand, and perhaps even influence, their behaviour.

It is up to you where to start but the most common starting point is in the operations domain where you work on the actual delivery, building up the high-level service design between the different layers that can be distinguished between the generic service delivery processes. You should begin with having a possible set of outputs and user mandatory and desirable requirements in mind. You probably need to begin by brainstorming and thinking about different possibilities.

In applying BSD, you can use the service blueprint as a scratch-pad for understanding the different attributes of the service under scrutiny during analysis and synthesis. A lot of information that becomes available can be saved in a repository for use later. In the next table you will find examples of questions to be asked in the different segments of the service blueprint template.

Table 4.1: Examples of questions asked in the service blueprint diagram

| | Specific | |
	Service delivery	Condition
Request/ user actions	• To whom are the services available?	• What will be the billing criteria? • How will licencing be handled? • Is training for users needed? Who is responsible for carrying out the training? • Are there specific needs concerning the availability of the service?
Interaction/ interface	• How is the product delivered by the provider? • Is there a point of contact (interface) for reporting functional calls (incidents, disruptions, questions, complaints)?	• How will identity and access regulations be applied? • Are there rules that limit or enlarge access to services?
Front office/ visible contact	• What activities does the provider undertake to supply the user with the product?	• How will an employee know which services are needed to do their job?

	Specific	
	Service delivery	**Condition**
	• Will there be a dedicated service desk and team? • Is training for agents necessary and which measures must be taken?	• Which communications activities must be taken?
Interaction/ interface	• Can requests be settled directly or should they undergo further processing? • How is the process between front and back offices tuned (agreements, cooperation, an authorised procedure or automated procedure)?	• Are there any mandatory rules according to job demarcation lines?
Back office/ invisible contact What control and monitoring of the activities should be taken? Back office/ interface	• How will accumulated data be stored, retrieved and used? • Do suppliers have capability to deliver the services? • What should the provider to the deliver?	• Are security demands met? • How will visually impaired people be enabled to use the apps? • How will 'knowledge' be accumulated and maintained? • Has anyone taken responsibility for the non-automated

	Specific	
	Service delivery	**Condition**
Back office/ support		elements of the service? <ul><li>Who will have overall responsibility for the service delivery?</li><li>Who will have overall responsibility for the technical development?</li><li>Who will have overall responsibility for the maintenance?</li><li>What resources are needed to implement user support?</li></ul>

	Generic questions delivery	Condition
Request/users actions	<ul><li>Where the Hell is the project charter…?</li><li>How will duplicated data be handled?</li><li>What will happen when</li></ul>	<ul><li>Which policy frames need to be in place?</li><li>What are the training plans and who owns them?</li><li>What are the identity and access regulations?</li></ul>
Interaction/ interface		
Front office/ visible contact		
Interaction/ interface		

	Generic questions delivery	Condition
Back office/ invisible contact What control and monitoring of the activities should be taken?	an employee leaves the organisation? • What will be the back-up (policies and plans)? • How will customer and user support be organised? • What is customer and user support? • Do I panic now? • Who is updating any corporate data that may be needed to transact business using the new services (for example securely held interest tables or actuarial models)? • How are changes	• How will the programme be audited? • What security policy is needed for this new service? • What communications issues can be determined? • Are there firm agreements in place about accepting changes/functional requirements and the processing of changes/ functional requirements? • Do contingency and recovery plans require additional agreements and instructions? • Must specific agreements about classification and storage of data be made? • Who is responsible for the policy framework?
Back office/ interface
Back office/ support

	Generic questions delivery	Condition
	addressed and how are they managed? • What arrangements must be made in the event of disaster recovery? • What dependencies has the proposed service with existing information services? • Who is examining the scope of the activities? • Who is making the list of risks and keeping track of mitigation or resolution? • Who is maintaining the project charter that we finally found?	• Are we compliant with privacy legislation? • Are we compliant with organisation policy? • How will they relate to current business applications/business portfolio? • What are the over-arching security policies? • Have you identified any issues about data integrity? • If so what are the risks related to the issues? • What are the capability requirements now and in the future? • Is a structure for issue and risk management for this service available? • What specific management measures should be taken for this service?

	Generic questions delivery	Condition
	• How will development be organised? • How will common but private information be secured? • How will availability be achieved?	

4.3 Transactions derive from actions and resources

To produce appropriate outcomes, transactions need to occur between different stakeholders. The different transactions are derived from activities and processes. These transactions, as we discussed, can be informational or physical. For example, a policy, an order, a demand, a communication, a delivery, disposal of an existing platform or website, rules, legislation, etc. To solidify these processes and activities (so they lead to viable transactions that can take place between stakeholder groups), the various stakeholders will need resources.[12] Resources comprise of capital (assets and money) and people:

---

[12] There are many definitions for 'processes' and 'activities'. We use Obers, G.-J. & Achterberg, K. (2014). Grip op processen in organisaties. Analyseren, ontwerpen en inrichten van bedrijfsprocessen. Zaltbommel: Van Haren Publishing.

- Capital assets may be machinery, applications, the workplace, buildings, cars, official documents, platforms, money, time, space, information, mandate, power, access to decision making, etc.
- People assets may be competences, capacity, knowledge, way of working, agents, etc.

These resources may be available and need to be used, or are not available and have to be acquired. Applying resources leads to activities and all the activities are then fused to shape processes. The processes instantiated will lead to the desired output. Clearly, by encouraging or discouraging the amount of resources applied, the output will be altered. Motivation to achieve an outcome (need and responsibility) leads to a desired output. Or, at least it should.

4.4 Risk management and compliance

In applying resources, you will encounter constraints and, therefore, experience potential risk (see Figure 4.4). Depending on the type of services that you wish to design, potential risk can be severe ranging from dangerous working environments or hazardous working materials, to freak accidents.

A certain amount of risk taking is inevitable, if your organisation is to achieve its objectives and deploy successful services. During the process of analysing the different requirements, you will find that applying resources can lead to risk. The service constellation helps you to identify these risks. Risk analysis is concerned with gathering information about exposure to risk so that later the enterprise can decide whether the risks that belong to the proposed architectural service design are acceptable and which appropriate measures must be in place to manage risk appropriately.

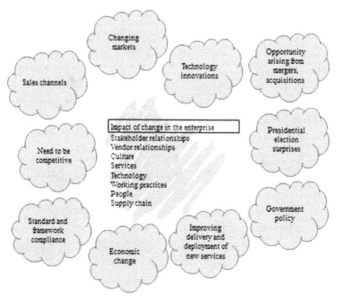

Figure 4.4: Potential risks of delivering services[13]

There are many useful tools, such as checklists, workshops, questionnaires and brainstorming to support risk identification. The use of techniques, prompt lists, questionnaires and interviews to gather information on the threats, helps to gain insight into the potential risks and agree their severity, or even propose ways of addressing them.

---

[13] OGC, (2002), Management of Risks: Guidance for Practitioners, Published by TSO for OCG Crown Copyright 2002.

4.5 Instruments for agreement

When we agree on the service offering, we need to draw up the necessary agreements between the stakeholders. This should be done to be clear who will be responsible for the different activities that must be in place to make the service offering a reality. So, for example, if we issue a Cloud service we must be sure that policy guidelines on data protection and privacy are in place. By capturing the different responsibilities that should be in place, the service offering can become reality.

It is necessary then that we bind the responsibilities that come from a specific set of transactions that make up all activities, deliveries, processes, exchanges, etc. which are part of the informational and physical transactions. These are called agreements; where the agreement is legally binding, it is a contract. An agreement can be judicial (contract), a management settlement (service agreement), a wish list for customers (a portfolio), or a promise to the users (catalogue). They sum up all the reasons why all different transactions between stakeholders take place and capture the total service process.

There are four types of agreements:

1. Policy (framework)
2. Service level agreement (internal)
3. Service catalogue
4. Contracts

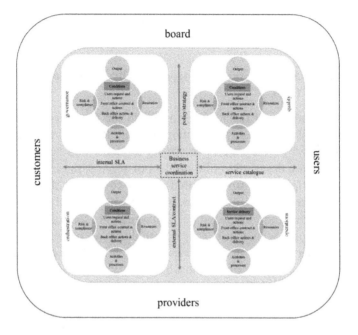

**Figure 4.5: BSD canvas with agreement on the axis,
risk's and transaction-items in each domain**

4.5.1 Policy

Between the board and business service coordination,
different information is flowing that can be summarised in
policy contracts, such as management contracts, principles
and guidelines. These will guide the BSC into establishing
agreements between the other stakeholders. Policy is often
misunderstood in IT; IT policies relate to technical,
operational issues whereas enterprise policies refer to much
wider issues, such as privacy, compliance, how lines of

business will deal with complaints from external customers, HR, and so on.

4.5.2 Service catalogue/product delivery catalogue (PDC)

The purpose of the PDC is to inform the users about the available services of the enterprise. The PDC is the 'shop window' of the enterprise for its products and services. Besides a description of a product or service, there is also a description of how and under what conditions the user can decrease the use of services and at what level of quality products and services are delivered. A service in a catalogue is one that exists; it should not be 'offered' if it is under construction, or to users not entitled to consume the service (some duties must be segregated, as must some services).

Today, the PDC is often made available through the intranet. In some cases, forms linked to the products and services are supplied so that users can not only refer to the PDC but also directly place an order *via* the intranet. The PDC is established based on SLAs, the experience of the staff of the service (and sales), in combination with the requirements of clear communication.

The PDC can serve multiple purposes and can act as:

- communication to customers (a window function)
- a marketing tool
- means to make transparent the added value of the facility organisation
- means for collecting and classifying information management

- instruction manual for employees of the service desk.

4.5.3   Service level agreements (internal)

While the PDC serves as a supply list for users, the internal service level agreement is a contract between the (top) management and service orchestrator. This contract lays down conditions under which the enterprise delivers its products and services. In a SLA, we generally find:

- the type of services delivered
- the level of performance achieved
- the conditions under which services are provided
- the availability and accessibility of the facility support
- the associated costs
- the available personnel
- how quality is guaranteed.

Because of its status, the internal SLA has a more formal language than the PDC. The SLA is less detailed and more formulated from the objectives of management. That means that products and services are provided from a vision associated with the business.

An internal SLA provides the tools to provide the required services, considering cost and quality control. Thus, the SLA also provides input for the formation, computation and the connection of the budget. By means of the basic service package and the associated work processes, we can determine a normative budget amount. Coupled with standard numbers, this forms the basis for the calculation of a normative formation.

In addition to products and services, the SLA defines the conditions that the service provider will offer the enterprise, in terms of mandate, the work to be performed, and the way complaints can be addressed.

4.5.4   Contracts

A contract is a legally binding instrument; ask anyone who ever signed one. A SLA is an agreement, but its terms and conditions have no legal obligation. If we fail to deliver then we might apologise, or we might not. Combining the service level agreement criteria within the contract is recommended if the SLA needs to be legally binding.

If we have signed a contract failure to deliver has legally enforceable penalties.

Within BSD, we distinguish between contracts that are legally binding and contracts between internal service providers and the BSC. In the latter case, it is up to the organisational units involved to dictate the level of detail required. We also differentiate between these SLAs and the SLAs created between the service orchestrator and customer. In situations with external parties, there is inevitably a legal obligation. In that case a contract, whether or not it's in the form of a written agreement, is the result of a multilateral legal act whereby one or more parties to one or more other parties undertake an obligation.

Be careful what you wish for. Your contract may impose a fine (a big one) on a service provider that fails to deliver, but money is not much use if the failure put you out of business because you could not recover lost sales.

4. Capabilities and Resources Within the Constellation

In the next chapter, we explain how to analyse the service constellation, aggregate the pieces together and derive the service design statement.

5. SERVICE DESIGN STATEMENT

All truths are easy to understand once they are discovered;
the point is to discover them.

Galileo Galilei

5.1 Business service design deliverable

In this chapter, we will reiterate the principal steps in BSD mentioned in Chapter two, focusing on the actual 'thing', the SDS that you must deliver. The result of the BSD session should be a design description encapsulated in a 'SDS'. It may not be the *best* service offering because the BSD deliverable is the most appropriate service offering. Service design thinking facilitates the enterprise in extensively checking this ideal service design offering and governing the development of the proposed service and innovation requirements. The design thinking approach will surface enough information in the design stage to influence design choices made and understand the capabilities needed. Therefore, the output is a description of a service offering, rather than the detailed design of the service offering.

The contents of the service design statement should, as a minimum, comprise:

General

- Service offering – description and justification of the service offering (output of the desired service design, outcome of the desired service design and

---

how output relates to outcome). You can explain the service offering based on the user story by explaining delivery, fit to policy and strategy, integration with the enterprise architecture and organisational and marketing objectives, and specific efficiency advantages.

- Customers and users – insight about motivations, needs and expectations (various actors involved in the target service are identified, their needs and responsibilities described).
- Managing delivery – how delivery of the service is to be managed and coordinated and any dependencies on support processes.
- Requirements for the service offering.
- Requirements for the complete service offering by all the stakeholders:
  o Operational – insight into system requirements, functional requirements, transaction and external interfaces.
  o Quality – attributes and features.
  o Governance – insight and requirements of business strategy, business information and business rules.
  o Requirements for orchestration (the requirements of the operating model).

Market and supplier

- How providers will be able to deliver the needed service offering.
- Whether and to what extent the service offering complies with market standards and commercial

off the shelf solutions (COTS) or if it is to be 'custom made'.

Risk management

- Insight into constraints and critical resources needed.
- Insight into the risks and understanding of countermeasures involved in managing risk.

The content of the SDS helps you to understand whether the overall design aligns with all operational, quality, governance and demand objectives within the domains.

Examples of questions that should be answered by the SDS:

- Is there a comprehensive, coherent description and justification of the service offering?
- Is there insight about motivations, needs and expectations of customers and users?
- How will the delivery of the service be managed and coordinated?
- Are there dependencies on support processes that must be managed/identified?
- Are all requirements explored, as stated by the stakeholders in the four domains?
- Are providers able to deliver the needed service offering?
- To what extent does the service offering comply with market standards and commercial off the

---

shelf solutions (COTS) or is it essentially to be 'custom made'?

- Are essential elements of contract and service agreement clear?
- Are constraints and critical resources identified?
- Are risks appreciated and understood and mitigations prepared?
- Are there particular issues that should be addressed in contracts to the providers?
- What are customer and user experience indicating?
- What are basic elements that should be part of the service level agreement?
- How will we communicate services and its procedures to the user?
- What essential policy agreements are set by the board?
- Are there particulars concerning how budget can be allocated to basic service and additional features?
- What are the legal issues that should be communicated in the agreements?
- Is there a business case or will the answers in the SDS be used to build the business case?

The position of the SDS in the service lifecycle (between business demand and the problem analysis and requirements analysis that leads to a detailed functional design (as shown in Figure 1.2). In other words, get it right before you go too far.

5.2   Putting the pieces together

By merging all the different transactions and underlying resources, a design should emerge.

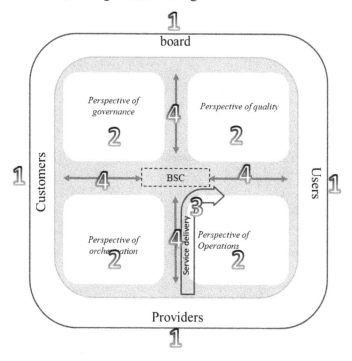

Figure 5.1: The four steps in the service constellation

Business service design follows four steps. The first step in the service constellation is explaining the type of questions asked by the different stakeholders, their need or responsibility, as is explained in Chapter three. In the second step, you identify the transactions that make up the requirement and conditions of the IT drivers and apply resources to construct transactions. The next step requires merging the transactions and domains in a service design. In addition, the needed transactions and resources can be summed up in an agreement between the stakeholders, as all is described here in this chapter.

The business service design is not complete until:

- All stakeholders are satisfied (with acceptance of the outputs and assurance of plausible outcomes).
- The necessary transactions are balanced and relevant compliances are in place.
- The extent of deployment of resources is clear and accepted.
- All corresponding risks have been assessed and addressed, and a risk management strategy is in place.

How do we know that the collective transactions lead to the desired output and are the building blocks of the business service we need? In general, one could say that if operations deliver, there is no further use to explore, because what you need is what you get.

Although, that is not perfectly true. In many enterprises, you will find that when a service is delivered, initially people get excited. But if a new service is not able to match the changing needs or easily adapt to a changing organisation, things start to go south. Were it only for delivering the service, then the transactions identified in the quality and operations domain should be enough to keep people satisfied. But remember our service lifecycle? Change is on us all the time and we need to blend the service within the enterprise policies and transformational needs.

Let's give you a simple example. If, based on best practice, policy dictates that large projects should be developed and delivered in small tranches, you must be careful to ensure that an overall big picture design exists, **but** that the whole shooting match is not delivered at one time. If you are not paying attention to policy change, you will probably find your enterprise mentioned in the newspaper as another project that has gone over time and budget.

5.3   Balancing in a favourable design

Remember our remark in section 4.2 about whether there are enough transactions to complete your IT-driven business service design? The integrated service constellation provides you with inbuilt checking mechanisms. The check to balance your service in a favourable design must answer the requirements set in the four domains. This leads to the need to answer four essential questions:

- Does it fit the delivery requirement (user journey, for example prototyping possible solutions)?
- Does it fit policy and strategy?
- Does it integrate with the enterprise architecture and organisational and marketing objectives?
- Does it fit efficiency needs?

In answering these four essential questions, you walk through the service constellation as pictured in Figure 5.2. Begin with the operations domain (the actual point of delivery) and progress anti-clockwise to the quality domain, governance domain and orchestration domain.

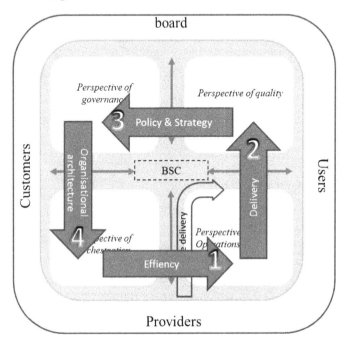

Figure 5.2: Completing the architectural service design story

Some thoughts in answering these questions:

- The success of a service offering is clear only when users are content with the service and are consuming the service. The service offering should be determined by understanding the experience of the user when they are actively involved in its operation.

- Furthermore, the service offering must be aligned with business goals and objectives. We indicated earlier that sometimes a service offering will not match certain policies, but is nevertheless consciously part of a business strategy, for example to gain market share. Validating these questions and perspectives is important for successful delivery. A more mundane reason for careful examination of policy versus need can be found in that service offerings are often developed from the perspective of a specific consensus by (general) management.

- In a market situation, the offering is part of a business model and, therefore, should be compliant with enterprise goals. If service offerings cost more than they make, that might not seem to be an effective use of resources. Of course, it may not always be a clear-cut situation. Sometimes offerings are part of a company's desire to offer a more complete portfolio and the enterprise will accept situations where offerings are financially less interesting (or even cost money) but lead to a more complete portfolio, or perhaps offer important added value.

- In non-profit situations, one can imagine that political goals and policy outcome far outweigh financial objectives. Sometimes, discussion revolves about the price of medicine compared to the price of a life. What is the cost at which a life-saving operation, or treatment with expensive medicine, will be declined? This question arises in national health services as well as insurance-driven services, such as that provided (or more often avoided) in the US.

- Next, you should decide whether the design aligns with organisational, architectural and marketing objectives. For example, will it suit existing contracts, are prospective new providers able to work within the enterprise eco-system, will the service offering fit marketing decisions, will the delivery make use of existing systems and so on?
- Finally, all of these perspectives (operations, quality, governance and orchestration) must be aligned in the most effective and efficient delivery of the service offering. Understanding these perspectives and exploring different strategies must lead to choices that not only satisfy stakeholders but also deliver a viable service design. This decision rule is known as 'satisficing'.[14] This should, of course, not imply that a solution that is acceptable to all participants but does not lead to the desired service provision will be accepted! And beware of compromise; compromises are often enforced with the result that no one is satisfied.

5.4 Using the SDS

Success depends on whether all the information is available to cover all the information in the design and development

---

[14] Satisficing; a strategy for decision making or cognitive heuristics that refers to a searching algorithm along different alternatives till an acceptable threshold has been reached. The approach is coined by Henry Simon in 1959. Simon, H.A. (1959), Theories of decision-making in economics and behavioural science, In: American economic review, vol. 49, issue 3 (June 1959), pp. 253–283.

stages. From a business point of view, you should have all the business information needed to justify further investment and sign-off. It is essential that the business understands that the service offering statement reflects the service they need, not necessarily the service they requested. It supports the balancing between customer intimacy and operational excellence.

The SDS should now be signed off by the SRO (not BSC!) or steering committee, whichever is responsible, and you are ready to go forward in your business service lifecycle. The SDS now specifies the essentials that need to be absolutely nailed down, and can be used as a guideline to focus the work to be done. It directs the choices and activities that must be in place to build, implement, maintain and execute the service delivery.

In Figure 5.3 some ideas are offered about the possible use for your SDS.

The primary value of the SDS is in evaluating service offering feasibility. It therefore is an essential part of the business case. In many instances, the statement will also serve as the starting point for the detailed design and development phase.

The SDS is the foundation for a request for information (RFI) or request for purchasing (RFP), potentially used, for example, in best-value purchasing. It can act as input for the supply to validate technical delivery perspectives and to identify more details to complete the design stage. In such instances, a comprehensive check focusing on whether providers can deliver the needed service offering is recommended.

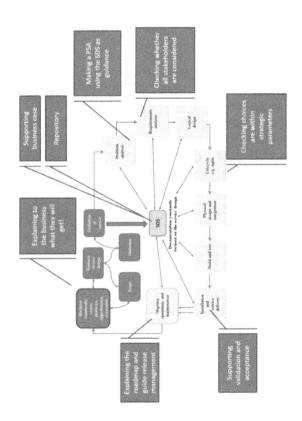

Figure 5.3: Practical use of the Service Design Statement

In earlier chapters, we surmise that the providers involved in our BSD sessions are always on hand. This is not always the case. It is imperative that we acknowledge that sometimes the right provider has not been involved, or that the necessary tasks are not assigned to the right providers. Thus, in the BSD sessions, it is always recommended that contract managers are involved because of their inside knowledge.

There are two principal issues that are frequently overlooked that will lead to problems later; first, the provider, whether they are involved in the initial BSD sessions or later in the development and delivery lifecycle, **must** have the capability to deliver. Second, it is possible that the desired solutions are beyond the level of technology available in the market. If your enterprise is the first to seek a particular technology solution, keep in mind that this is a risk as well as an opportunity. NASA might see an opportunity with flights to Mars, even if technology is new and not tested. However, the preference is likely to be to create a modern webstore or information web portal using proven technology and standards, and focus principally on the desired outcome.

Early in the design process, it must be clear whether the service offering should comply with standard solutions. The advantages of standard solutions are that prices tend to be more reasonable because of economies of scale for the providers, and because there is competition.

5.5   One final thing: managing the BSC

BSC is the key role in navigating the service constellation. BSC retains responsibility for referencing the SDS throughout in the service development lifecycle. The BSC, remember, has the responsibility to bind the transactions together to make sure the service offering is effective. We can list the tasks (Table 5.1) relating to the different activities and accompanying processes. This can be used as a guideline and described differently in any enterprise.

When no BSC exists (whatever you name it) you must allocate the BSC responsibilities to the different departments or units within your enterprise. The BSC can be instantiated in numerous ways and we consider the role within BSD could be conceptual, to assign to it all the activities and responsibilities that cannot be (directly) allocated to the four other stakeholders. We could decide that for each service offering (or LoB) there is a separate BSC. Or we could decide that all service offerings are managed within one BSC. Secondly, a BSC might be one department, or the responsibility of one person, or alternatively, all the tasks of BSC may be dispersed over different departments.

We again stress that there is no absolute right or wrong. There can be many reasons why a specific type of design or configuration is chosen. And often we find hybrid situations where some service offerings are under one BSC and other service offerings are managed by a collective of departments or organisational units. Nevertheless, a choice for one configuration has consequences. For example, if a task for one service offering is dispersed within the enterprise, coordination, control and innovation will be more difficult than specific tasks brought under one responsibility.

Table 5.1: Tasks of the business service coordination

	Customer base and need	Service offering	Performance management	Creation and delivering needed services
Delivery of the service offering	• Relation and account management • Service catalogue • Analysis of need • Customer satisfaction	• Strategy • Portfolio management • Architectural design • Service integration	• Management and control (financial, judicial) • Analysis • Risk management	• Operational contract management • Quality assurance • Supplier management

AFTERWORD

Business is driven by IT. You need to get over this fact. When the time comes to improve the business services provided by IT, or to create new services, business discussions about service requirements often wander into a detailed analysis of current business procedures, followed by a discussion about procurement, leading directly into the acquisition of a solution that really does not fit the desires and needs of the business.

This situation arises because at the start of such discussions (that are often lengthy and complex) the senior responsible owner (SRO) becomes overwhelmed and loses sight of the essential issues and principles that are needed to guide the full IT-driven business service lifecycle. Pressure to improve quickly leads to action that is not properly assessed. The SRO (or their proxy) needs to be able to intervene the moment that such developments arise. Of course, many SROs are able to make interventions, though numerous overspends or failures to deliver IT programmes or projects, or the revision of the expected benefits of new services, all provide evidence to the contrary.

In our experience, we find that most issues relating to poor design could be identified early in the planning lifecycle. Often, the moment the discussion between demand and supply begins, the understanding gets lost in words, ideas and perceptions. We think business people understand IT and we think IT people understand business – but they do not. And both sides proceed with a design on the basis that any problems will be addressed as they arise, which leads to a costly exercise in changing things as they develop, which further results in major delays or (ultimately) cancellations.

These initial discussions between the demand side and the supply side should be held early, before any analysis and development of the essential components of the business design moves forward. Only then can the SRO be satisfied that the outcomes will be what is required by the business. In this way we accelerate the translation of the needs of the business to the delivery of IT intensive business services. Overall, you reduce the time spent over the entire spectrum of design, develop, build, test, go back to square one, and tear out your hair life cycles, leading to faster time to market and more strategic agility. And guess what? You ensure that you build and deliver IT-driven business services that are fit for use and the aforementioned SRO does not get grief from the Board!

ITG RESOURCES

IT Governance Ltd sources, creates and delivers products and services to meet the real-world, evolving IT governance needs of today's organisations, directors, managers and practitioners.

The IT Governance website (*www.itgovernance.co.uk*) is the international one-stop-shop for corporate and IT governance information, advice, guidance, books, tools, training and consultancy. On the website you will find the following page related to the subject matter of this book: *www.itgovernance.co.uk/itsm*.

Publishing Services

IT Governance Publishing (ITGP) is the world's leading IT-GRC publishing imprint that is wholly owned by IT Governance Ltd.

With books and tools covering all IT governance, risk and compliance frameworks, we are the publisher of choice for authors and distributors alike, producing unique and practical publications of the highest quality, in the latest formats available, which readers will find invaluable.

www.itgovernancepublishing.co.uk is the website dedicated to ITGP. Other titles published by ITGP that may be of interest include:

- Governance of Enterprise IT based on COBIT 5
  www.itgovernance.co.uk/shop/product/governance-of-enterprise-it-based-on-cobit-5
- Running IT like a Business - A step-by-step guide to Accenture's internal IT
  www.itgovernance.co.uk/shop/product/running-it-like-a-business-a-step-by-step-guide-to-accentures-internal-it
- Assessing IT Projects to Ensure Successful Outcomes
  www.itgovernance.co.uk/shop/product/assessing-it-projects-to-ensure-successful-outcomes

We also offer a range of toolkits that give comprehensive, customisable documents to help users create the specific documentation they need to properly implement a management system or standard. Written by experienced practitioners and based on the latest best practice, ITGP toolkits can save months of work for organisations working towards compliance with a given standard.

Please visit *www.itgovernance.co.uk/shop/category/itgp-toolkits* to see our full range of toolkits.

Training Services

The IT Governance training programme is built on the foundations of our extensive practical experience of designing and implementing management systems. Our training courses offer a structured learning path from Foundation to Advanced level for IT practitioners and lead implementers, and help to develop the skills needed to deliver best practice and compliance in an organisation. In addition they provide the tools for career advancement via industry standard certifications and increased peer recognition.

Our key training sectors include:

- Information security
- PCI DSS compliance
- Business continuity
- IT governance
- Service management
- Professional certification

For further information please visit *www.itgovernance.co.uk/training*.

Professional Services and Consultancy

IT Governance is a world leader in the field of IT GRC (governance, risk management and compliance) solutions. Our multi-sector and multi-standard knowledge and experience can accelerate your projects, wherever you are in the world.

Our mission is to engage with business executives, senior managers and IT professionals, and to help them protect and secure their intellectual capital, comply with relevant regulations and thrive as they achieve strategic goals through better IT management.

We have a wide range of consultancy delivery methods, guaranteed to suit all budgets, timescales and preferred project approaches.

We're independent of vendors and certification bodies, and encourage our clients to select the best fit for their needs and objectives. For general information about our consultancy services, including for ISO 27001, ISO 20000, ISO 22301, Cyber Essentials, the PCI DSS, data protection and more, please see *www.itgovernance.co.uk/consulting*.

Daily Sentinel

Want to stay up-to-date with the latest developments and resources in the IT GRC market? We will send you mobile-friendly emails with fresh news and features about your preferred areas of interest, as well as unmissable offers and free resources to help you successfully start your projects. *www.itgovernance.co.uk/daily-sentinel*.

Branded Publishing Services

ITGP's wide range of titles provide information governance, risk management and compliance (IT GRC) expertise from renowned industry practitioners.

If you're taking advantage of our expert knowledge in your organisation, you can now customise our titles with your own branding thanks to our Branded Publishing Service. For more information, please visit *www.itgovernancepublishing.co.uk/publishing-services.aspx*.

EU for product safety is Stephen Evans, The Mill Enterprise Hub, Stagreenan, Drogheda, Co. Louth, A92 CD3D, Ireland. (servicecentre@itgovernance.eu)

www.ingramcontent.com/pod-product-compliance
Lightning Source LLC
Chambersburg PA
CBHW070841070326
40690CB00009B/1651